Student Book 1

SERIES EDITORS
JoAnn (Jodi) Crandall
Joan Kang Shin

AUTHOR
Diane Pinkley

Unit 0		2
Unit 1	My Classroom	8
Unit 2	My World	24
Unit 3	My Family	40
Units 1–3 Review		56
Unit 4	My House	58
Unit 5	Cool Clothes	74
Unit 6	My Toys	90
Units 4–6 Review		106
Unit 7	My Body	108
Unit 8	Good Food	124
Unit 9	Animal Friends	140
Units 7–9 Review		156
Our World song		158
Cutouts		159
Stickers		

Australia • Brazil • Japan • Korea • Mexico • Singapore • Spain • United Kingdom • United States

Unit 0

Welcome to Our World!

Eddie
the elephant

Polly
the parrot

Mia
the monkey

Freddy
the frog

1 **Look and listen.** Say. TR: A2

Colors

2 **Look and listen.** Say. TR: A3

3 **Listen.** Point and say. TR: A4

4 **Work with a partner.** Point. Ask and answer. TR: A5

What color is it?

It's red!

The Alphabet

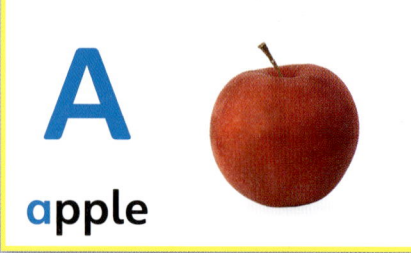
A apple

B baby

C cat

G goat

H hand

I ice cream

M monkey

N nine

O orange

S sock

T turtle

U umbrella

Y yellow

Z zebra

 **D** **d**og

 **E** **e**gg

 **F** **f**ish

 **J** **j**acket

 **K** **k**ite

 **L** **l**amp

 **P** **p**encil

 **Q** **q**ueen

 **R** **r**obot

 **V** **v**egetables

 **W** **w**ater

 **X** fo**x**

5 **Look and listen.** Say. TR: A6

6 Look and listen. Say. TR: A7

a square   a triangle   a circle   a rectangle   a star

7 Listen. Point and say. TR: A8

8 Look and listen. Say. TR: A9

1	2	3	4	5
one	two	three	four	five

6	7	8	9	10
six	seven	eight	nine	ten

9 Listen. Point and say. TR: A10

10 Ask and answer. TR: A11

How many blue squares?

Three.

 draw
 listen
 point
 read
 say
 sing
 sit down
 stand up
 walk
 write

11 **Look and listen.** Say. TR: A12

12 **Listen.** Point and say. TR: A13

13 **Listen and do.** TR: A14

Unit 1
My Classroom

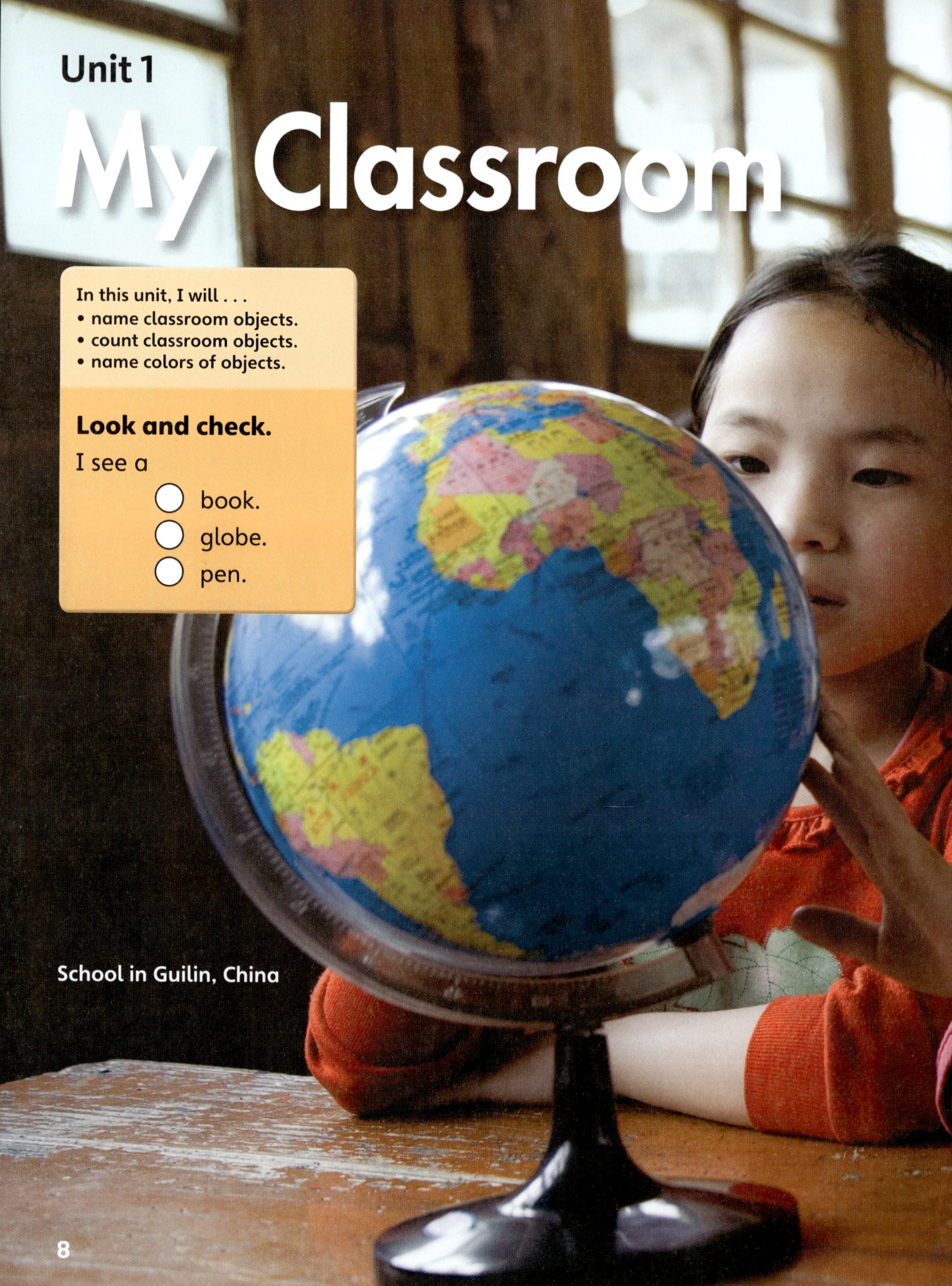

In this unit, I will . . .
- name classroom objects.
- count classroom objects.
- name colors of objects.

Look and check.

I see a
- ◯ book.
- ◯ globe.
- ◯ pen.

School in Guilin, China

1. **Listen and say.** TR: A15

2. **Listen.** Point and say. TR: A16

4 Listen. Read and sing. TR: A18

My School

This is my school.
This is your school.
This is my school.
I like my school.

I have my eraser,
and I have my book.
I have my eraser.
Come and look!

CHORUS

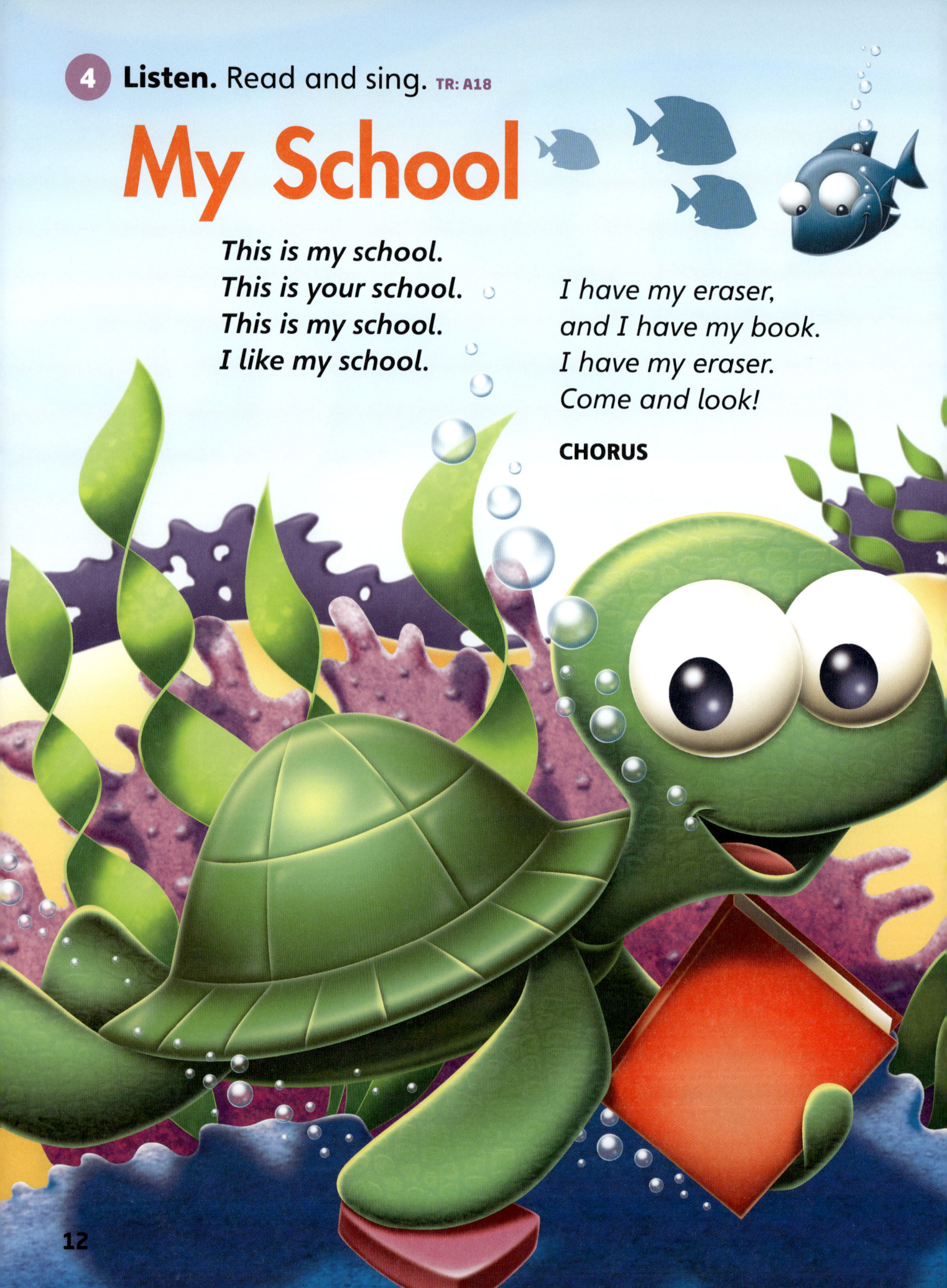

We can count from one to ten.
Just like this, just like this.

Is everybody ready?
Here we go!
1-2-3-4-5-6-7-8-9-10
Yay!

CHORUS

I know my colors.
Red and blue,
purple, too.
Orange, green, and yellow!

CHORUS

I like my school!

5 **Sing again.** Hold up pictures.

GRAMMAR TR: A19

Is it a pencil? Yes, **it is.** **It's** a pencil.
Is it a crayon? No, **it isn't.** **It's** a pen.

6 **Look.** Listen and (circle.) TR: A20

1

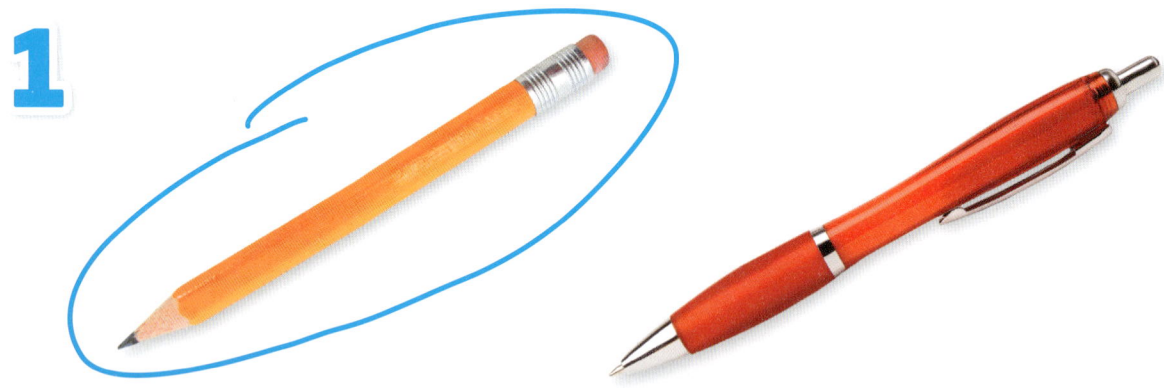

2

3

 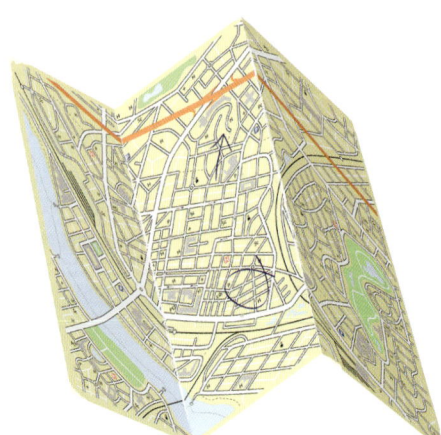

15

7 **Listen and say.** TR: A21

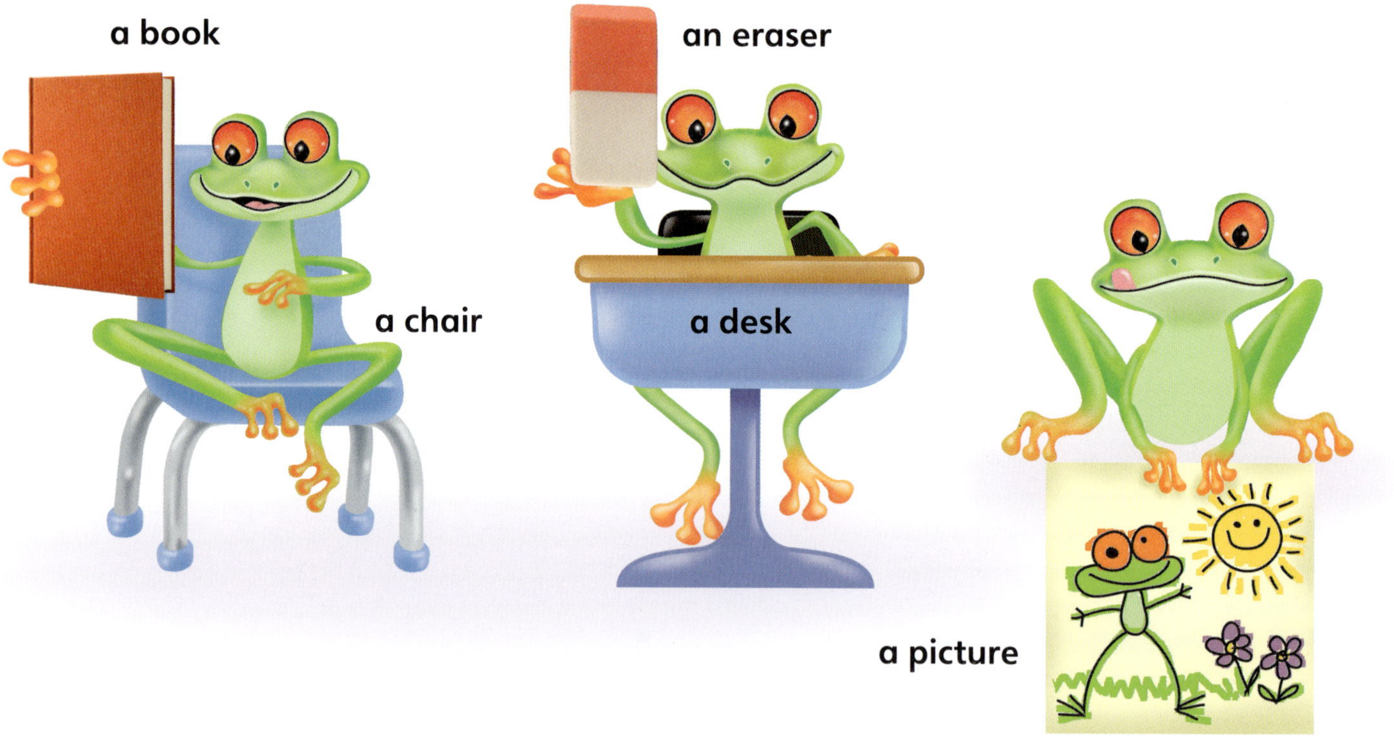

a book   an eraser

a chair   a desk

a picture

8 **Work with a partner.** Point and say.

9 **Work with a partner.** Guess and stick. TR: A22

Is it a desk?

No, it isn't.

Is it a book?

Yes, it is.
It's a book.

1   2   3   4   5

GRAMMAR TR: A23

What is it?	It's a table.
What color is it?	It's yellow.
How many pencils?	Three.

What color is it?

It's yellow.

10 Work in groups. Look and point. Ask and answer. TR: A24

11 Look at the picture. Write.

1. How many crayons? _____

2. What color is the frog? _____

3. How many clocks? _____

12 Listen and read. TR: A25

Drawing and Writing

Cueva de las Manos, Argentina

a wall

a hand

a tablet

a stick

In the past

Now

a canvas

paint

a tablet

13 What about you? Circle.

1. I draw on   **a wall**   **paper.**
2. I draw with   **a crayon**   **a stick.**
3. I write with   **a hand**   **a pencil.**

14 Work with a partner. Look and read. Check. ✔

	Past	Now
crayon		✔
hand		
paint		
tablet		
stick		

15 Look in your desk. Read. Count and write.

1. How many frogs? ___0___
2. How many pencils? _____
3. How many crayons? _____
4. How many sticks? _____
5. How many pens? _____

Zero!

16 Make a name tag.

1. Cut out the name tag on page 159.
2. Write **Hello** with a crayon.
3. Write **My name is** with a pencil.
4. Write your name in a different color.

17 Put on your name tag.
Walk and talk. TR: A26

Hello. My name is Mia. What's your name?

Hi. I'm Freddy.

NATIONAL GEOGRAPHIC
Our World
Work hard in school.

18 **Look and read.**

I listen. I talk.
I read. I write.

19 **Read and copy.**

I work hard in school.

20 Make a counting book.

Cut out the pictures on page 159.

Decide how many.

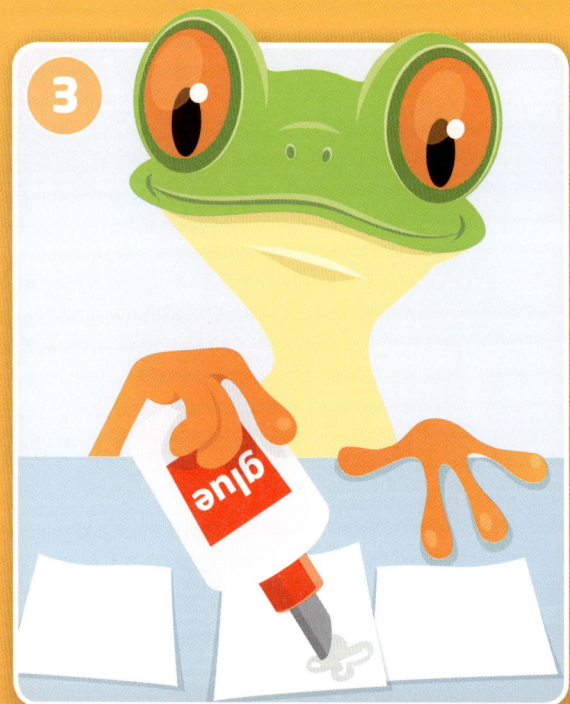
Color and glue the pictures.

Draw more pictures and write the number.

Unit 2
My World

In this unit, I will . . .
- name objects in nature.
- name colors in nature.
- talk about nature.

Look and check.

The boy has a
- ○ frog
- ○ bird
- ○ bug

on his finger.

1 **Listen and say.** TR: A27

2 **Listen.** Point and say. TR: A28

the sun
the sky
grass
the ocean
a bird
a rock

4 **Listen.** Read and sing. TR: A30

Nature

Where are the birds?
They're in the sky.

Where are the sun and the moon?
They're in the sky.

The sky is part of our world.

Where are the fish?
They're in the ocean.

Where are the waves?
They're in the ocean.

The ocean and the sky
are part of our world.

Where are the trees?
They're in the mountains.

Where are the rocks?
Up in the mountains.

The mountains and the ocean
and the sky, they're part of our world.

*What colors do you see
in our beautiful world?
What colors do you see
in our beautiful world?*

*The colors of the rainbow,
the colors of the rainbow.
The colors of the rainbow,
the colors of the rainbow.*

*The rainbows and the mountains
and the ocean and the sky,
they're part of our world,
part of our world.*

Our beautiful world!

5 **Sing again.** Hold up pictures.

GRAMMAR TR: A31

What **is** it? It**'s** a bird.
What **are** they? They**'re** birds.

6 **Look.** Listen and (circle.) TR: A32

1

2

7 Listen and say. TR: A33

a star

a cloud

the moon

a flower

a bush

8 Work with a partner. Point and say.

9 Work with a partner. Guess and stick. TR: A34

Is it a bush?
No, it isn't.
Is it a butterfly?
Yes, it is.

1   2   3   4   5

GRAMMAR TR: A35

Where is the butterfly?   It's **on** the flower.
Where are the clouds?   They're **in** the sky.

10 Play with a partner. Ask and answer. TR: A36

Where are the clouds?

They're in the sky.

11 Look at the pictures. Write.

1. How many birds? _____

2. What color are the flowers? _____

3. Where are the stars? _____

33

12 Listen and read. TR: A37

Rainbows

The sun is in the sky. Rain is in the sky. Look! A rainbow! A rainbow is red, orange, yellow, green, blue, indigo, and violet.

13 Listen and read. (Circle) yes or no. TR: A38

1. For a rainbow, the sun is in the sky.   yes   no
2. Ten colors are in the rainbow.   yes   no

14 **Color the rainbow.**

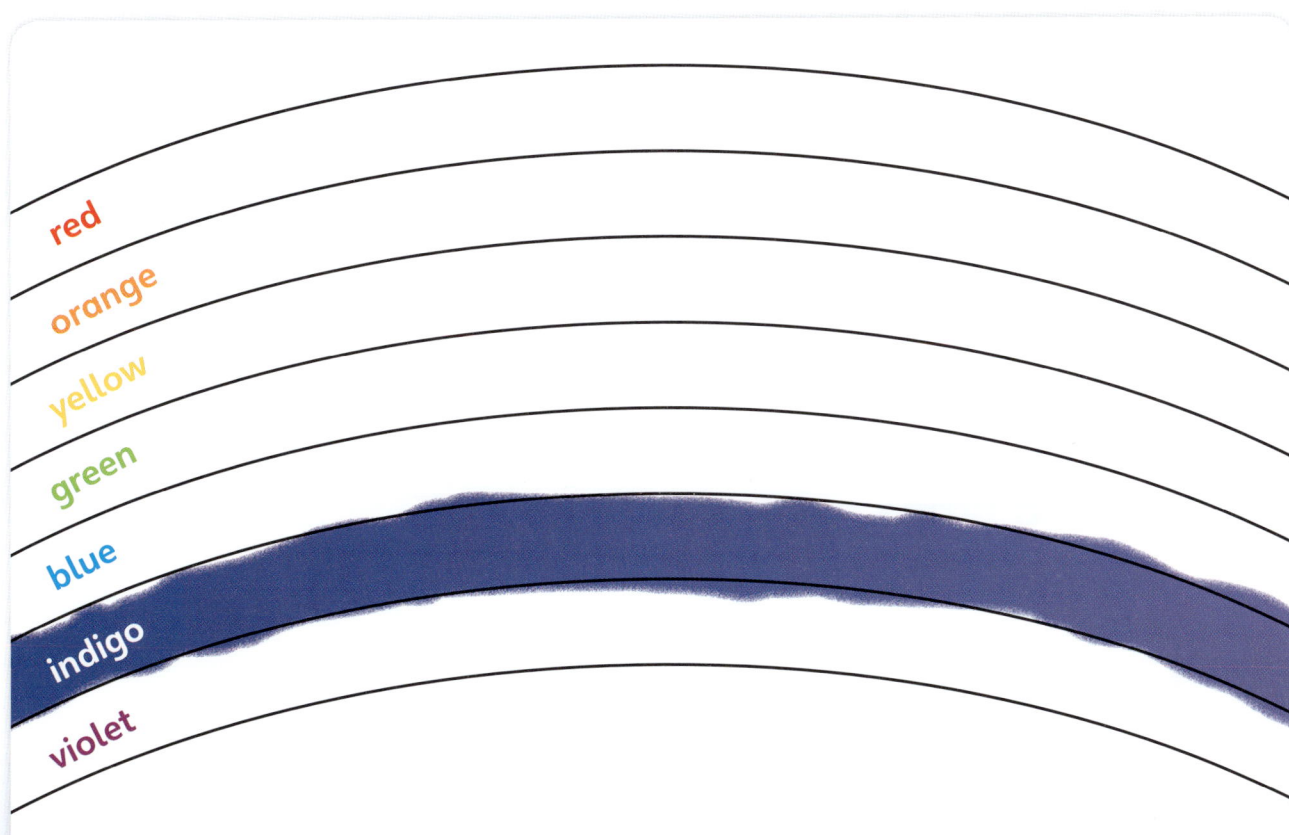

red
orange
yellow
green
blue
indigo
violet

15 **Look.** Circle **things in the sky. Say.**

The bush is green.
The flowers are red, yellow, and blue.
The birds are red and black.

16 **Color and write.**

1. The tree is _____.

2. The _____ is _____.

3. The flowers are _____.

4. The _____ are _____.

17 **Work in a group.** Talk about your picture.

NATIONAL GEOGRAPHIC

Our World

Enjoy nature.

18 Look and read.

Stop and look.
Enjoy.

Wadi Bani Khalid, Oman

19 Read and copy.

I look at the trees and flowers. I enjoy nature.

20 Make a mural about nature.

Cut out the pictures on page 161.

Draw more pictures.

Glue things from nature.

Write your name.

Unit 3
My Family

In this unit, I will . . .
- name family members.
- talk about family members.
- use numbers.

Look and check.
There are
- ○ three
- ○ four
- ○ five

people in this family.

Bryce Canyon National Park, USA

4 Listen. Read and sing. TR: A42

Big or Small?

Do you have a big family?
Do you have a big family?
Do you have a big family?
Yes, my family is big!

Do you have a little brother?
Do you have a little sister?
Do you have a little baby
in your family?

I don't have a little brother,
little sister, baby brother.
My brother is big!

Some are short, and some are tall.
I have a big family, and I love them all!

How many people are in your family?
How many people are in your family?
How many people are in your family?
Two, three, four, five or more?

There are two boys in my family.
There are two girls in my family.

There are six people in my family.
And I love them all!

Some are short, and some are tall.
I have a big family, and I love them all!

My family is big.
Your family is small.

I love the people in my family!
Yes, I love them all.
I love them all!
I love them all!

5 **Sing again.** Hold up pictures.

GRAMMAR TR: A43

How many brothers **do** you **have**?   I **have** two brothers.
How many sisters **do** you **have**?   I **don't have** any sisters.

6 **Look and listen.** Draw a line. TR: A44

Julia

Dao

Ryan

Aisha

7. Listen and say. TR: A45

8. Work with a partner. Point and say.

9. Work with a partner. Listen. Say and stick. TR: A46

Number 1. The grandfather is old.

Yes, he's old. My turn.

1   2   3   4   5

GRAMMAR TR: A47

Who's she?   She's my sister. She's nine.
Who's he?   He's my grandpa. He's old!

10 **Play a game.** Cut out the pictures on page 163. Glue. Listen and play. TR: A48

11 **Look at the pictures.** Write *yes* or *no*.

1. Is the grandpa old? _____

2. Is the mother tall? _____

3. Is the brother young? _____

49

12 Listen and read. TR: A49

Families Are Different

This family from Turkey is small. There are parents and a boy.

This family from Mexico is big. There is a grandfather, a grandmother, a father, and a mother. There are four brothers and one sister.

13 Listen and read. Draw a line. TR: A50

1. The family from Mexico   has three people.
2. The family from Turkey   has nine people.

14 Look at this family tree. Write.

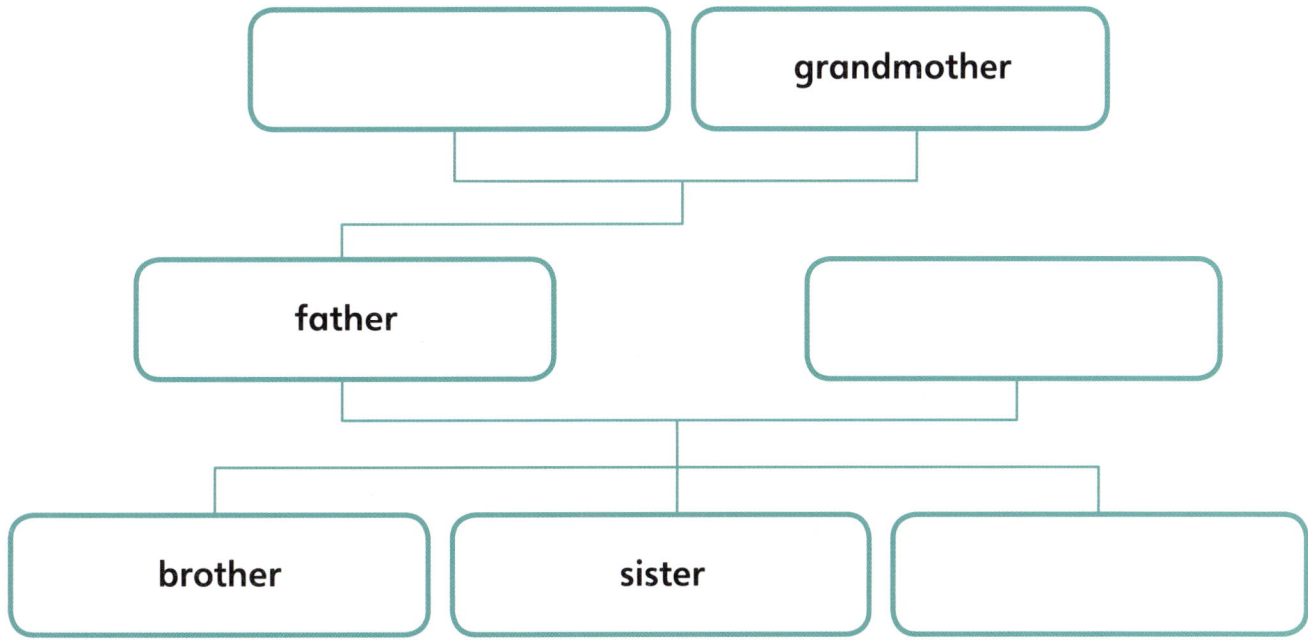

15 Work with a partner. Ask and answer. Write.

My family is big.

	You	Your Partner
Name		
Family Size		
Brothers		
Sisters		

51

I'm Adrian. I have a big family. In this photo, you see my grandfather, my grandmother, my parents, and my other grandmother. I have one sister and one brother. In this photo, I am the baby!

16 **Draw and write.**

I'm _____. I have a _____.

In this picture, you see my _____.

I have _____.

17 **Work in a group.** Talk about your picture.

52

NATIONAL GEOGRAPHIC

Our World

Love your family.

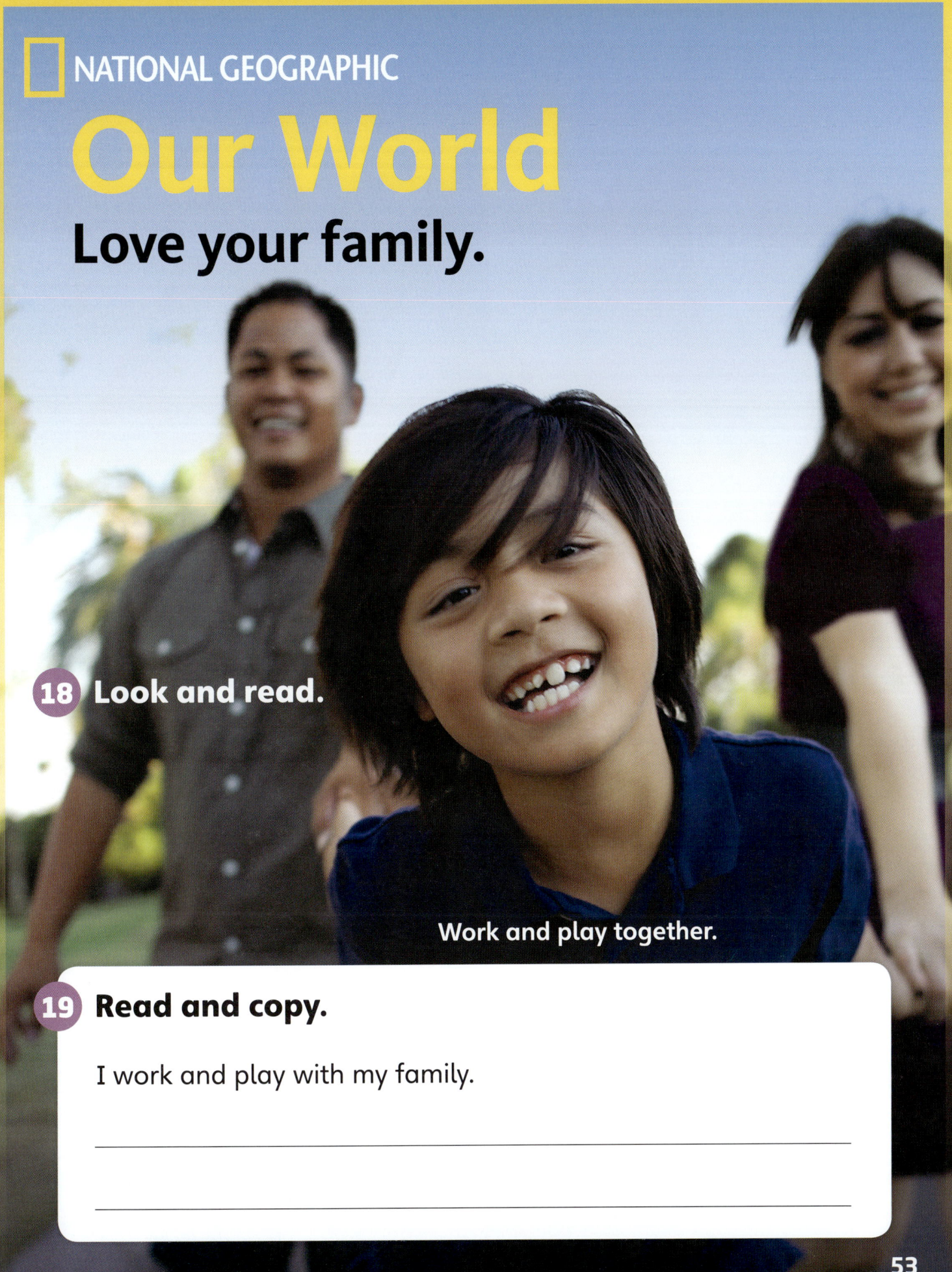

18 **Look and read.**

Work and play together.

19 **Read and copy.**

I work and play with my family.

_____

_____

20 Make a family photo poster.

Cut out the frame on page 163. Draw more frames.

Choose photos.

Glue photos and frames.

Write.

Review

Start

Heads = 1 space
Tails = 2 spaces

Unit 4

My House

In this unit, I will . . .
- name rooms in a house.
- name furniture.
- talk about actions.

Look and check.

The house is
 big.
 small.

Drina River, Serbia

1 **Listen and say.** TR: A51

2 **Listen.** Point and say. TR: A52

4 Listen. Read and sing. TR: A54

My Home

Where do you live?
I live in an apartment.
Where do you live?
I live in a house.

Where do you sleep?
I sleep in the bedroom.
Is there a bed?
Yes, there is.

At home, my home,
at home, where I live.

Where do you eat?
I eat in the kitchen.
Is there a spoon?
Yes, there is.

Where do you play?
I play in the backyard.
Is there a ball?
Yes, there is.

At home, my home,
at home, where I live.
It's where I live!

5 **Sing again.** Hold up pictures.

GRAMMAR TR: A55

Is there a table in the kitchen? Yes, **there is.**
Is there a sofa in the kitchen? No, **there isn't.**

6 **Look.** Listen and check. ✔ TR: A56

1. ◯ yes ◯ no   4. ◯ yes ◯ no
2. ◯ yes ◯ no   5. ◯ yes ◯ no
3. ◯ yes ◯ no   6. ◯ yes ◯ no

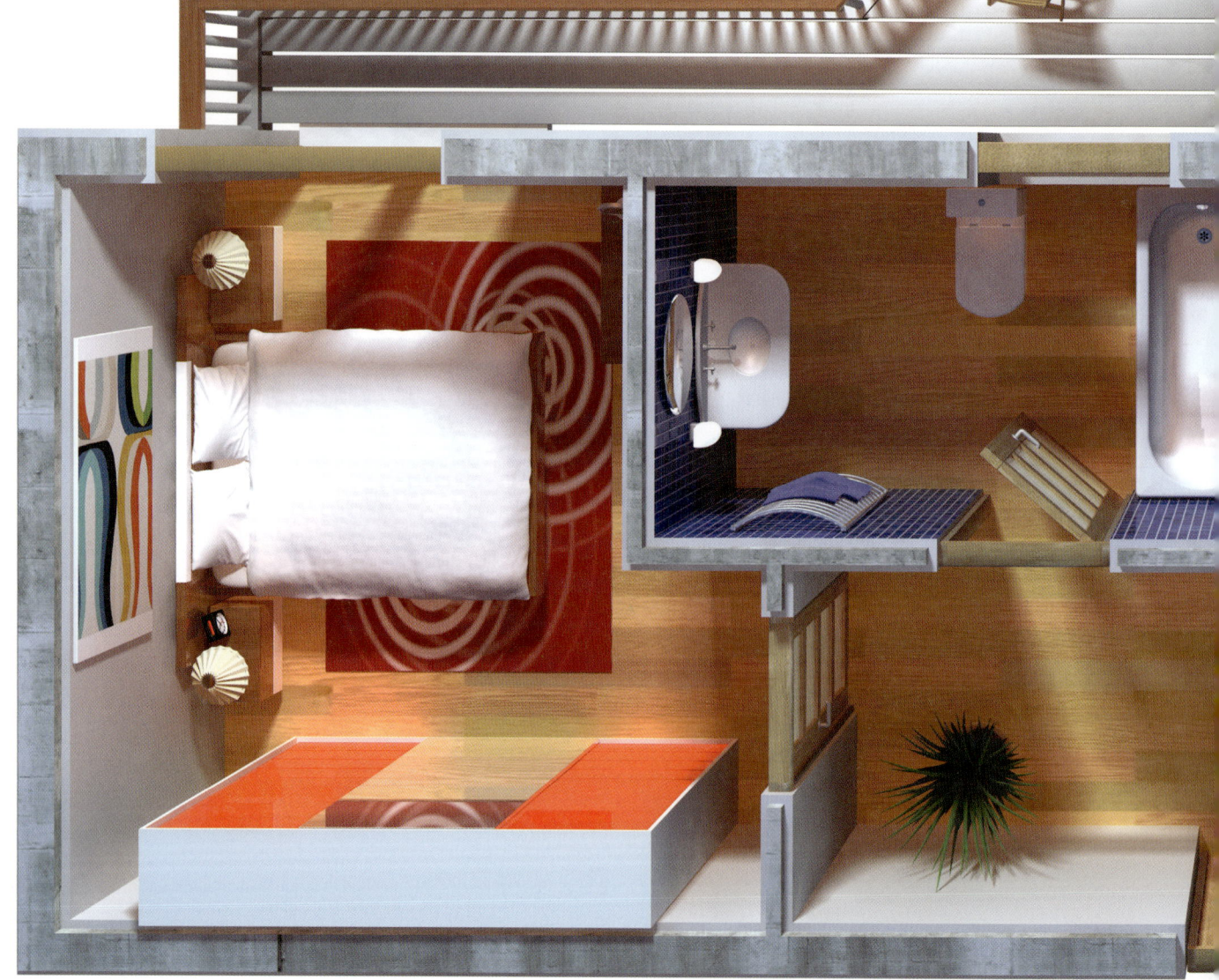

64

7 **Listen and say.** TR: A57

sleeping

cleaning

cooking

taking a bath

eating

watching TV

8 **Work with a partner.** Point and say.

9 **Work with a partner.** Listen. Say and stick. TR: A58

Number 1. He's cooking.

Ok. My turn. Number 2.

1　2　3　4　5

GRAMMAR TR: A59

Where's your mother? She's in the kitchen. She**'s cooking.**
Where's your brother? He's in the living room. He**'s watching TV.**

10 **Play a game.**
Point. Ask and answer. TR: A60

Where's the frog?

He's in the dining room. He's eating.

11 **Look at the pictures.** Write.

1. How many frogs are there? _____

2. What color is the sofa? _____

3. Where is the TV? _____

12 Listen and read. TR: A61

Houses Are Different

Most houses have kitchens, living rooms, and bedrooms inside, but the outside of houses can be very different.

Is there a house here?

a houseboat

Kerala, India

13 Listen and read. Look. Circle. TR: A62

1. Some houses are on the water.   yes   no
2. Most houses have kitchens.   yes   no

14 **Look at the shapes.** Draw a line.

1. circle

2. rectangle

3. square

4. triangle

15 **Look at the houses.** What shape are they? Draw a line.

1. circle   2. rectangle   3. square   4. triangle

16 **What shape is your house?** (Circle.)

circle   rectangle   square   triangle

I'm Teddy. This is my bedroom. My bed is blue. I have a red rug under my bed. There is a lamp on a small table.

17 Draw and write.

I'm _____. This is _____.

My _____ is _____.

I have _____.

There is _____.

18 Work in a group. Talk about your picture.

NATIONAL GEOGRAPHIC
Our World

Be neat.

19 Look and read.

Be neat.
Clean your room.

20 Read and copy.

I am neat. I clean my room.

21 **Make a plan of rooms in a house.**

Cut out the pictures on page 165. Draw more pictures.

Organize the pictures.

Glue the pictures.

Write your name.

Unit 5

Cool Clothes

In this unit, I will . . .
- name clothes.
- name colors.
- say what people are wearing.

Look and check.

Her clothes are
- ○ red.
- ○ white.
- ○ blue.

Guatemalan girl

1 **Listen and say.** TR: B2

2 **Listen.** Point and say. TR: B3

a hat
gloves
a skirt
a jacket

Guilin, China

4 **Listen.** Read and sing. TR: B5

My Clothes

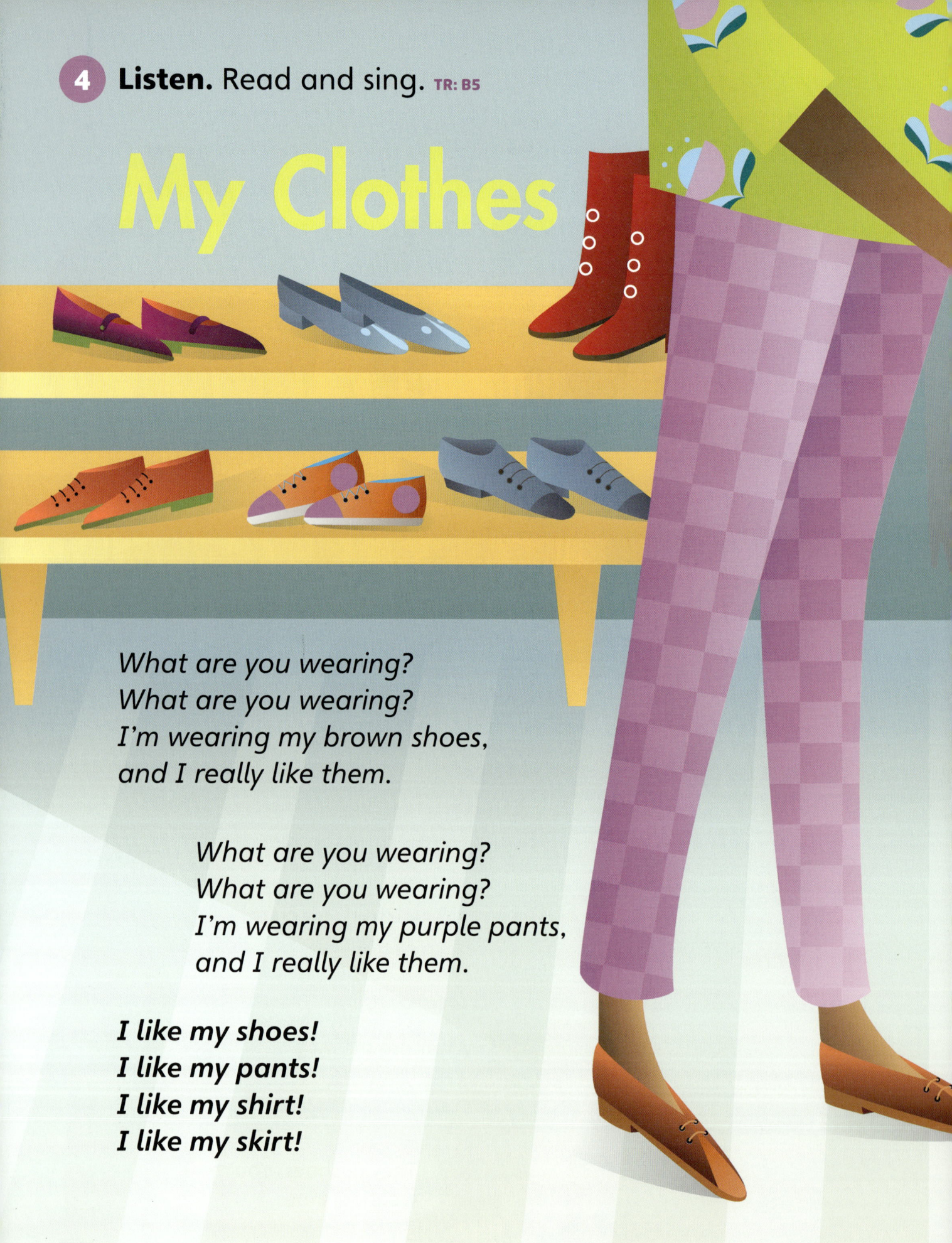

What are you wearing?
What are you wearing?
I'm wearing my brown shoes,
and I really like them.

What are you wearing?
What are you wearing?
I'm wearing my purple pants,
and I really like them.

I like my shoes!
I like my pants!
I like my shirt!
I like my skirt!

What are you wearing?
What are you wearing?
I'm wearing my orange shirt,
and I really like it.

What are you wearing?
What are you wearing?
I'm wearing my pink skirt,
and I really like it.

CHORUS

Oh, you look nice.
Thank you.
Nice hat.
Nice shoes.
Nice shirt.

5 **Sing again.**
Hold up pictures.

GRAMMAR TR: B6

What **are** you **wearing?** I**'m wearing** a red dress.
My sister**'s wearing** a green dress.

6 **Listen and find.** Color. TR: B7

80

7 **Draw and color.** What are you wearing? Talk. TR: B8

What are you wearing?

I'm wearing a blue T-shirt.

8 Listen and say. TR: B9

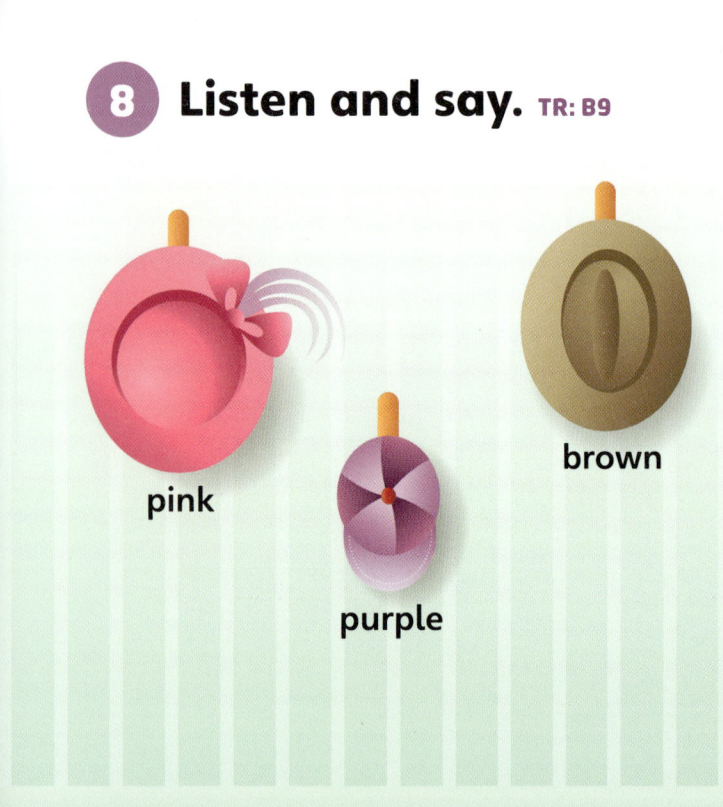

pink

purple

brown

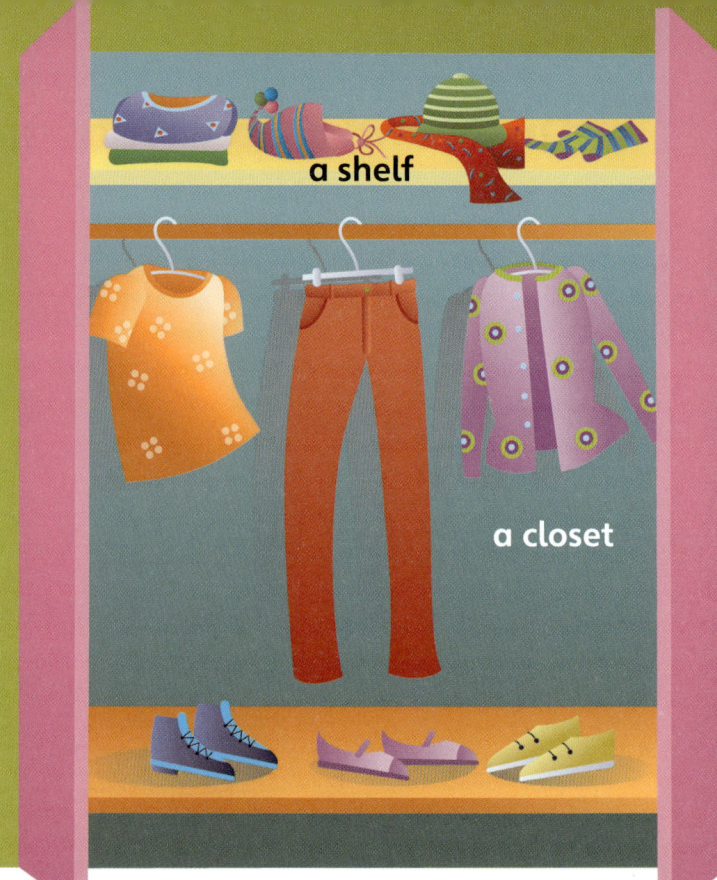

a shelf

a closet

9 Work with a partner. Point and say.

10 Listen and read. Circle. TR: B10

1. Is there a black hat?   yes   no
2. Is there a purple hat?   yes   no

11 Work with a partner. Listen. Say and stick. TR: B11

Where's the green hat?

It's on the shelf. My turn.

1   2   3   4   5

GRAMMAR TR: B12

What's that?   That's my orange T-shirt.
What are those?   Those are my purple shoes.

12 Play a game. Ask and answer. Draw lines. TR: B13

13 Look at the pictures. Write.

1. What color are the gloves? _____

2. What color is the hat? _____

3. Is there a jacket? _____

14 **Listen and read.** TR: B14

Clothes Are Fun!

People all over the world wear special clothes on special days. Sometimes they are clothes from the past.

15 **Listen and read.** Look. (Circle) *yes* or *no*. TR: B15

1. The children from Turkey are wearing shoes.   yes   no
2. The girls from Korea are wearing dresses.   yes   no

16 Look at Activity 14. Check ✔ the costume colors.

	from **Turkey**	from **Peru**	from **Korea**		from **Turkey**	from **Peru**	from **Korea**
black				pink			
blue				purple			
brown				red			
green				yellow			
orange				white			

17 Look. Draw a line.

1. hat
2. jacket
3. pants
4. shirt
5. dress

Spain

18 Work with a partner. What are you wearing today? Ask and answer. TR: B16

What are you wearing?

I'm wearing a white shirt, blue pants, and black shoes.

85

The girl is wearing a red shirt and a black and red skirt. The boy is wearing a white shirt, a blue jacket, and brown pants.

19 **Color and write.**

The girl is wearing _____.

The boy is wearing _____.

20 **Work in a group.** Talk about your picture.

NATIONAL GEOGRAPHIC

Our World

Take care of your clothes.

21 Look and read.

Put away your clean clothes.

Mandawa, India

22 Read and copy.

I take care of my clothes.

23 Dress a stick puppet.

Cut out the pictures on page 167.

Choose a head.

Glue the clothes.

Glue the puppet to the stick.

Unit 6

My Toys

In this unit, I will . . .
- name and describe toys.
- talk about wants.
- talk about possession.

Look and (circle).

The toys are

blue   green

red   yellow

black   pink

Santa Fe, New Mexico

1 **Listen and say.** TR: B17

2 **Listen.** Point and say. TR: B18

a train

a drum

Tokyo, Japan

a bike

a ball

4 Listen. Read and sing. TR: B20

Let's Play!

Do you want to play?
Do you want to play with me?
Do you want to play?
Do you want to play with me?
Do you want to play?
Do you want to play with me?
Yes, I do! Yes, I do!

Do you want to bang on a drum?
No, I don't.
Do you want to ride a bike?
No, I don't.
Do you want to fly a kite?
Yes, I do.
I want to fly my kite with you!

**There is a shelf on the wall,
a box on the shelf,
toys in the box.
Toys for girls and boys!**

Do you want to dress my doll?
No, I don't.
Do you want to kick a ball?
No, I don't.
Do you want to play with trains?
Yes, I do.
I want to play with you!
Choo choo choo!

CHORUS

Let's play!

5 **Sing again.** Hold up pictures.

GRAMMAR TR: B21

Do you **want** a kite?   No, I **don't**.
Do you **want** a puppet?   Yes, I **do**.

6 **Listen and find.** Draw a line. TR: B22

GRAMMAR TR: B23

Does she **want** a ball?   Yes, she **does**.
Does he **want** a ball?   No, he **doesn't**. He **wants** a truck.

7 **Listen and circle.** TR: B24

1. Yes, he does. He wants a train.

   No, he doesn't. He wants a drum.

2. Yes, she does. She wants a puppet.

   No, she doesn't. She wants a car.

3. Yes, he does. He wants a game.

   No, he doesn't. He wants a kite.

4. Yes, she does. She wants a top.

   No, she doesn't. She wants a ball.

8 Listen and say. TR: B25

a robot

a teddy bear

a puzzle

a board game

a doll

9 Work with a partner. Point and say.

10 Listen and read. Circle yes or no. TR: B26

1. Does he want a robot?   yes   no
2. Does he want a puzzle? yes   no

11 Work with a partner. Listen. Say and stick. TR: B27

Number 1. I have a board game.

I don't. I have a robot. Number 2.

1   2   3   4   5

GRAMMAR TR: B28

Is this your teddy bear? No, **it** isn't. It's Sonia's teddy bear.
Are these your puppets? No, **they** aren't. They're Mark's puppets.

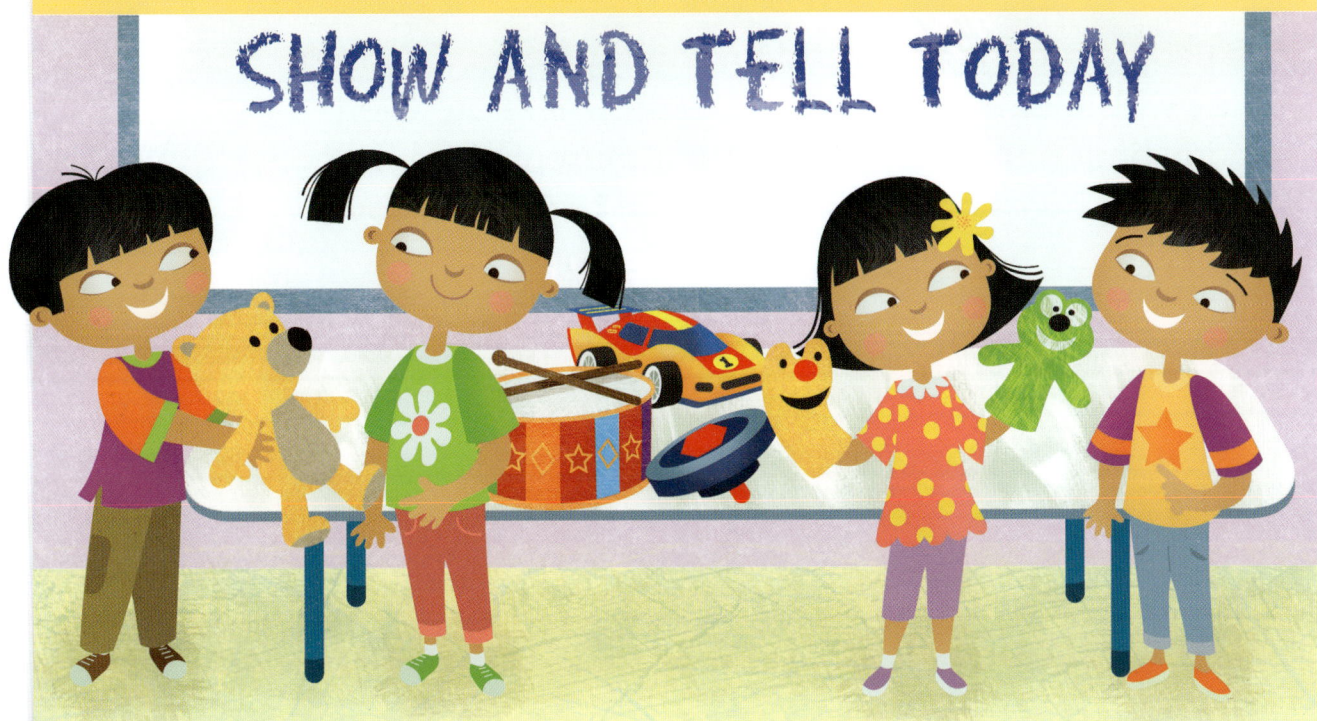

12. **Look.** Listen and read. Check ✔ *yes* or *no*. TR: B29

   yes   no
1. Is this Anna's puzzle? ○ ○
2. Are these Ken's robots? ○ ○

13. **Play a game.** Cut out the cards on page 169. Ask and answer. Play with a partner. TR: B30

Are these your tops?

No, they aren't. They're Tina's tops.

14 Listen and read. TR: B31

We ♥ Teddy Bears

People around the world love teddy bears. Children play with them and sleep with them. There are even teddy bear museums! This popular museum is in Korea. It has big bears and small bears, girl bears and boy bears. There are teddy bears for everyone!

15 Listen and read. Circle yes or no. TR: B32

1. There are teddy bear museums.   yes   no
2. This museum is in China.   yes   no
3. It has big bears and small bears.   yes   no

16 Look and write.

1. How many teddy bears are small? _____
2. How many are big? _____
3. How many colors are the bears? _____
4. How many have shirts? _____

17 Work with a partner. What are your favorite toys? Ask and answer. TR: B33

What are your favorite toys?

My teddy bear and my drum.

My favorite toy is my doll.
Her name is Kate. She is small.
She is wearing a pink dress.
I play with her in my bedroom.
She sleeps with me in my bed.

18 **Draw and write about your favorite toy.**

My favorite toy is _____

_____

_____

19 **Work in a group.** Talk about your picture.

NATIONAL GEOGRAPHIC
Our World

Share your toys.

20 **Look and read.**

Share your toys with your friends.

21 **Read and copy.**
I share my toys with my friends.

22 Make a cup-and-ball toy.

Decorate your cup. Write your name.

Make a hole in the bottom of the cup.

Pull string through the hole. Tie and tape the string.

Fix the string to a small ball. Play!

Review

Start

Heads =
1 space

Tails =
2 spaces

Work with a partner.
Look. Ask and answer.

Finish

Ask a question!

Where's the bed?

Unit 7
My Body

In this unit, I will . . .
- name parts of the body.
- talk about parts of the body.
- talk about actions.

Look and check.

This is
- ○ a doll.
- ○ a boy.
- ○ a girl.

Boy with face painted for a folk dance, Kolkata, India

4 Listen. Read and sing. TR: B37

My Body

My body, my body!
It's fun to move my body!
My body, my body!
Can you dance with me?

Legs, legs. Move your legs.
Legs, legs. Move your legs.
Legs, legs. Move your legs.
Can you walk with me?

Feet, feet. Move your feet.
Feet, feet. Move your feet.
Feet, feet. Move your feet.
Can you jump with me?

CHORUS

Mouth, mouth. Move your mouth.
Mouth, mouth. Move your mouth.
Mouth, mouth. Move your mouth.
Can you sing with me?

Hands, hands. Move your hands.
Hands, hands. Move your hands.
Hands, hands. Move your hands.
Can you clap with me?

CHORUS

My body, my body!
I love to move my body!
My body, my body!
Can you dance with me?

5 **Sing again.**
Hold up pictures.

GRAMMAR TR: B38

My hair is brown. **My** eyes are brown.
Your hair is brown. **Your** eyes are brown.

6 **Look and listen.** Write the number in the box. TR: B39

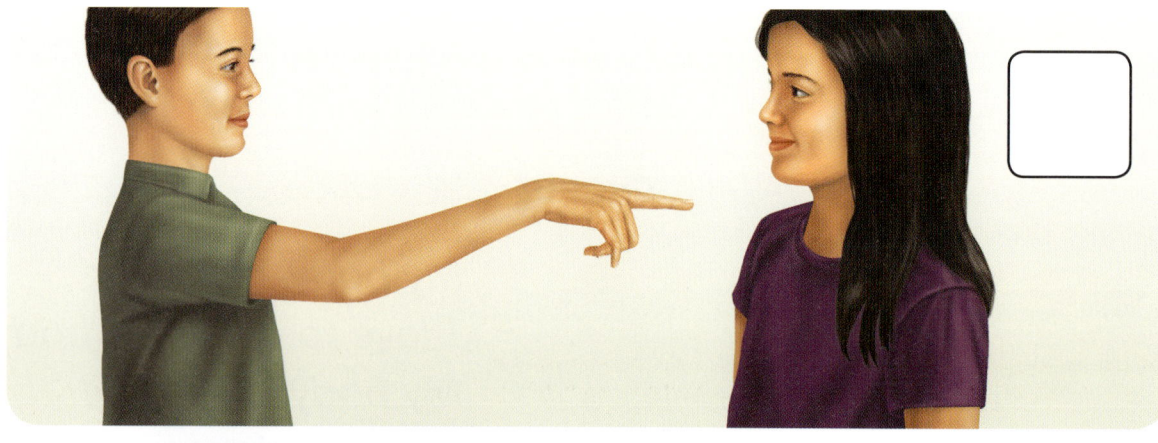

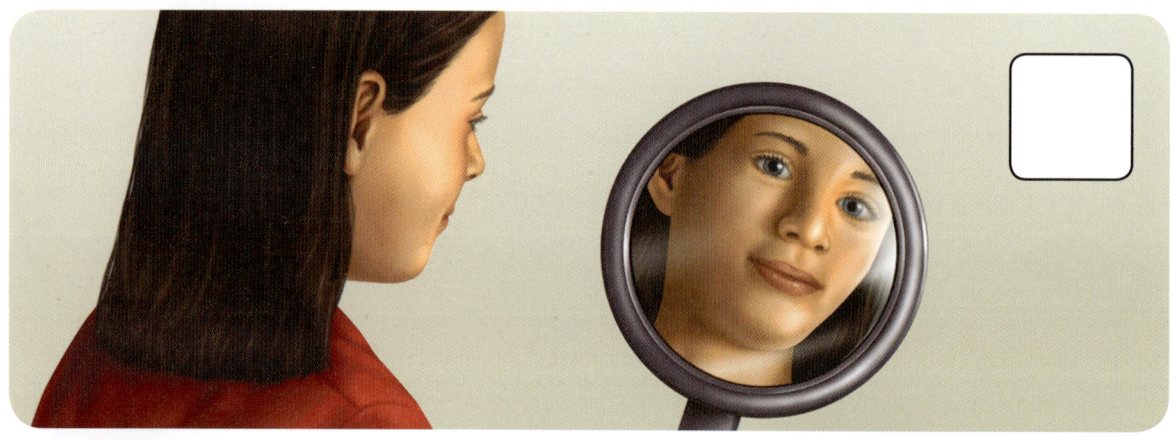

GRAMMAR TR: B40

His hair is brown.   **His** eyes are brown.
Her hair is brown.   **Her** eyes are brown.

7 Look and listen. Draw a line. TR: B41

1. Her ears are small.
2. His feet are big.

115

8 Listen and say. TR: B42

long hair · strong arms · run · walk · jump

9 Work with a partner. Point and say.

10 Work with a partner. Say and stick. TR: B43

Number 1. His legs are long.

Yes, they're long. My turn.

1 2 3 4 5

GRAMMAR TR: B44

I **can** walk. She **can** jump.
Can you run? Yes, I **can**. I have strong legs!

11 **Play a game.** Cut out the pictures on page 171. Glue. Listen and play. TR: B45

12 **Look at the pictures.** Write *yes* or *no*.

1. Can the boy run? _____

2. Can the baby jump? _____

3. Can the mother cook? _____

13 Listen and read. TR: B46

Sculptures Are Fun

Some artists draw and paint. Some artists make sculptures. They make people and animals. Look at the man with a hat. His arms and legs are big. His horse's head is small. Look at the balloon dog. Its legs are big. Its ears are long. Artists can make many fun things!

Fernando Botero's *Man on Horse*

Jeff Koons' *Balloon Dog*

14 Listen and read. (Circle.) TR: B47

1. There are **two three** sculptures.

2. Some arms and legs are **big. old.**

3. We can see a dog with **long short** ears.

15 Read and check ✔.

MAN	legs	arms
big	✔	
small		

DOG	legs	ears
big		
long		

16 Look. Circle and write.

1. My robot   **doesn't have**   (**has**)   hair.

   It   **doesn't have**   (**has**)   __1__ head.

   It   **doesn't have**   **has**   _____ eyes.

2. My robot   **doesn't have**   **has**   ears.

   It   **doesn't have**   **has**   _____ big hands.

   It   **doesn't have**   **has**   _____ short legs.

3. My robot   **doesn't have**   **has**   _____ eyes.

   It   **doesn't have**   **has**   _____ long arms.

   It   **doesn't have**   **has**   _____ leg.

17 Work with a partner. Choose a robot. Talk about your robots. Are your robots the same or different?

I'm Antoni. I have two eyes, one nose, and one mouth. I have two arms and two legs. I like spiders. My spider costume has eight eyes and eight legs. I'm a cool spider!

18 **Draw a costume and write.**

I'm _____. I have _____.

I have _____.

My _____ costume has _____

_____.

19 **Work in a group.** Talk about your picture.

NATIONAL GEOGRAPHIC

Our World

Be clean.

20 Look and read.

Wash your hands.
Wash your body.
Brush your teeth.

21 Read and copy.

I wash my body. I am clean.

_____

_____

22 **Make a robot.** Work with a partner.

Cut out the body.

Cut out a card.

Write the numbers.

Cut out or draw parts. Glue them.

Look! Our robot has two heads!

Now I can . . .

○ name parts of the body.

○ talk about parts of the body.

○ talk about actions.

Unit 8
Good Food

In this unit, I will . . .
- name food.
- talk about likes and dislikes.
- talk about my favorite food.

Look and check.

She sells
- ○ flowers.
- ○ fruit.
- ○ vegetables.

Kasbah, Rabat, Morocco

1 **Listen and say.** TR: B48

2 **Listen.** Point and say. TR: B49

a banana

cheese pizza

a salad

an apple

an orange

4 Listen. Read and sing. TR: B51

Yes, Please!

Pizza?
I like pizza!
Yes, I do! Yes, I do! Yes, I do!
I like pizza!
Yes, I do!
I like it very much!

Apples?
I like apples!
Yes, I do! Yes, I do! Yes, I do!
I like apples!
Yes, I do!
I like them very much!

Do you want a cookie?
Do you want some cheese?
Do you want a banana?
Yes, please!

Chicken?
I like chicken!
Yes, I do! Yes, I do! Yes, I do!
I like chicken!
Yes, I do!
I like it very much!

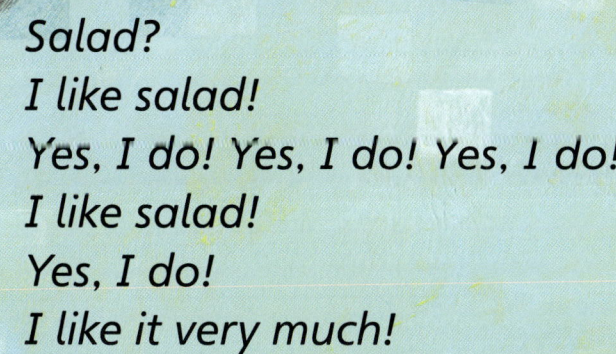

Salad?
I like salad!
Yes, I do! Yes, I do! Yes, I do!
I like salad!
Yes, I do!
I like it very much!

CHORUS

Oranges?
I like oranges!
Yes, I do! Yes, I do! Yes, I do!
I like oranges!
Yes, I do!
I like them very much!

Water?
And I like water!
Yes, I do! Yes, I do! Yes, I do!
I like water!
Yes, I do!
I like it very much!

CHORUS

Yes, please!
Yes, PLEASE!

5 **Sing again.**
Hold up pictures.

GRAMMAR TR: B52

Do you **like** apples?   No, I **don't**. I **don't like** apples.
Do you **like** bananas?   Yes, I **do**. I **like** bananas.

6 **What do they like?** Listen and find. Circle and write. TR: B53

1. _____   2. _____   3. _____

130

GRAMMAR TR: B54

Do you **like** fish? No, I **don't**. I **don't like** fish.
Do you **like** chicken? Yes, I **do**. I **like** chicken.

7 **What do they like?** Listen and find. Circle and write. TR: B55

1. _____ 2. _____ 3. _____

131

8 Listen and say. TR: B56

tea   orange juice   water   lemonade   milk

9 Work with a partner. Point and say.

10 Listen and read. Circle *yes* or *no*. TR: B57

1. Does she like orange juice?   yes   no
2. Does he like water?   yes   no

11 Work with a partner. Say and stick. TR: B58

132

GRAMMAR TR: B59

an apple   **an** egg   **an** orange   **a** banana   **a** cookie   **a** sandwich

12 Play a game. Play with a partner. Find and say. Draw lines. TR: B60

Look! It's an apple.

That is an apple, too.

13 Look at the pictures. Write.

1. Is there a frog? _No, there isn't a frog._

2. Is there an orange? _____

3. Is there a sandwich? _____

4. Is there an eraser? _____

133

14 Listen and read. TR: B61

Fun Food

Every day, people eat food. Every day, people play. Some people play with food! They make pictures of people or animals from fruits and vegetables. Some make sculptures. Many people like to make animals. Some of these animals look real, and some animals look like they are from stories. Some food sculptures look like toys. These are all examples of fun food. Just don't eat them!

You can eat everything in this picture!

15 **Listen and read.** Look. Circle *yes* or *no*. TR: B62

1. People can make sculptures with food.   yes   no
2. People don't make animals with food.   yes   no
3. Some animals look real.   yes   no

16 **Match.**

cookie

orange

apple

banana

17 **Look at the photo on page 134.** Write.

1. Are there any trees? _____
2. Are there any people? _____
3. Are there any houses? _____
4. Are there any clouds? _____

18 **Work with a partner.** Ask and answer.
What are your favorite foods? TR: B63

What are your favorite foods?

Chicken and pizza.

I eat my favorite foods at lunchtime and at night. For lunch, I like soup, a cheese sandwich, or a chicken sandwich. For dinner, I like salad, fish, and rice. I like to drink water or lemonade.

19 **Draw and write about your favorite foods.**

My favorite foods are _____

_____

_____.

20 **Work in a group.** Talk about your picture.

136

NATIONAL GEOGRAPHIC

Our World

Eat good food.

21 **Look and read.**

Eat fruits and vegetables.
Drink water and juice.

Cedar waxwing eating berries

22 **Read and copy.**

I eat fruits and vegetables. I drink water and juice.

_____

_____

23 Make a placemat.

Cut out the pictures on page 173.

Glue the pictures.

Decorate and draw.

Write your name.

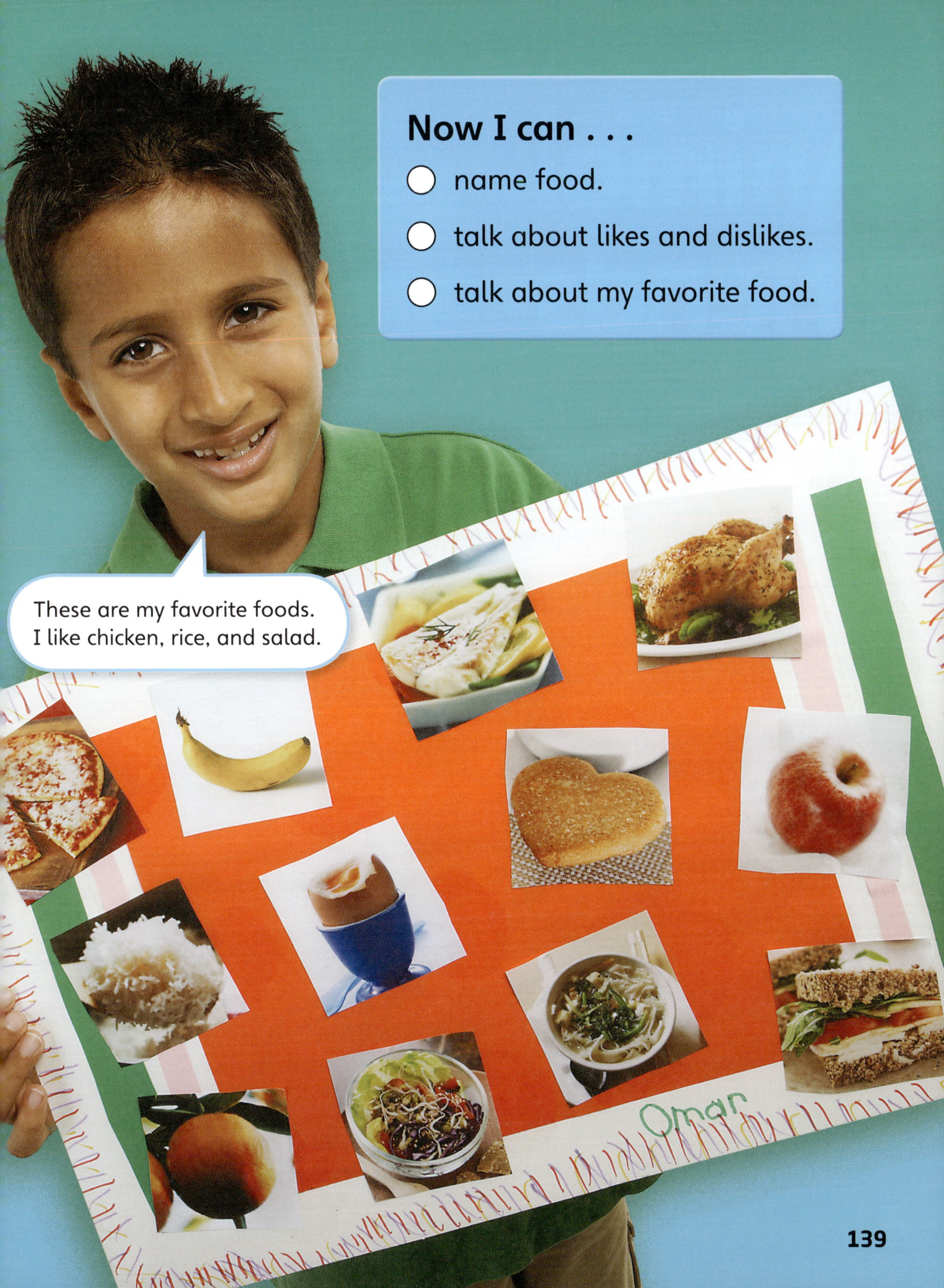

Now I can . . .
○ name food.
○ talk about likes and dislikes.
○ talk about my favorite food.

These are my favorite foods. I like chicken, rice, and salad.

Unit 9
Animal Friends

In this unit, I will . . .
- name animals.
- talk about what animals can do.
- describe a favorite animal.

Check T for *True* and F for *False*.

1. There's a monkey and a cat.   T   F
2. The monkey likes the bird.   T   F
3. The bird is green.   T   F
4. The monkey is a baby.   T   F

Macaque monkey and dove,
Neilingding Island, China

1. **Listen and say.** TR: B64

2. **Listen.** Point and say. TR: B65

a dog

a turtle

a cat

a frog

a duck

a horse

a goat

a cow

a chicken

a rabbit

a sheep

a donkey

3 **Work with a partner.**
Point. Ask and answer. TR: B66

What is it?

It's a donkey.

143

4 Listen. Read and sing. TR: B67

Animals

I see animals.
What are they doing?
I see animals.
Can you see them, too?

What do you see?

I see one dog.
Is it running?
Yes, it's running.
It's running in the sun.

What do you see?

I see two cats.
Are they climbing?
Yes, they're climbing.
They're climbing, and it's fun.

Running and climbing,
hopping and singing.
These are things we like to do.

Are you ready?
All together!

Run! Climb! Hop! Sing!

What do you see?

I see three frogs.
Are they hopping?
Yes, they're hopping.
They're hopping on a rock.

What do you see?

I see four birds.
Are they singing?
Yes, they're singing.
They're singing la, la, la!

La lalala!
La lala!

Running and climbing,
hopping and singing.
These are things we like to do.

Are you ready?
All together!
Run! Climb! Hop! Sing!

5 **Sing again.** Hold up pictures.

GRAMMAR TR: B68

What **are** the horses **doing**? They**'re running**.

6 **Listen and find.** Write. TR: B69

1. _____ 2. _____

3. _____ 4. _____

GRAMMAR TR: B70

Are they **sleeping?** No, they **aren't.**
Are they **eating?** Yes, they **are.**

7 **Listen and find.** Circle. TR: B71

1. sleeping   walking
2. jumping   eating
3. talking   reading
4. sleeping   jumping

147

8. Listen and say. TR: B72

see

climb

fly

swim

crawl

9. Work with a partner. Point and say.

10. Look. Listen and read. (Circle) yes or no. TR: B73

1. The birds are flying.   yes   no
2. The cat is swimming.   yes   no
3. The turtle is crawling. yes   no

11. Work with a partner. Listen. Say and stick. TR: B74

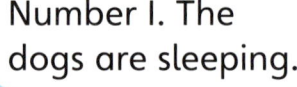

Number 1. The dogs are sleeping.

OK. Number 2.

1   2   3   4   5

148

GRAMMAR TR: B75

Do you **want to ride** the donkey?
What **do** you **want to do**?
What **does** Anna **want to do**?

No, I don't.
I **want to ride** the horse.
She **wants to see** the ducks.

12 **Look.** Listen and read. Write. TR: B76

1. Maria _____ the sheep.

2. Carlos _____ the frog.

13 **Play a game.** Cut out the cards on page 175. Ask and answer. Play with a partner. TR: B77

Do you want to see the goats?

No, I don't. I want to see the cows.

14 Listen and read. TR: B78

Animal Babies

Who loves babies? Everyone! Let's learn about some animals and their babies. Some animals have big families. Cats have many baby cats, called kittens. Baby dogs are called puppies. Baby chickens are called chicks. Baby rabbits are called bunnies. Some animals, like sheep and elephants, have small families. Baby sheep are called lambs. A baby elephant is called a calf. Everyone loves animal babies!

Baby Asian elephant

15 **Listen and read.** Circle *yes* or *no*. TR: B79

1. A baby rabbit is called a bunny.   yes   no
2. A baby sheep is called a chick.   yes   no
3. A baby elephant is called a calf.   yes   no

16 **Read and write.**

Animal Families

cat	dog	chicken	rabbit	sheep	elephant
↓	↓	↓	↓	↓	↓

17 **Look and write.**

1. How many kittens? _____
2. Are there any puppies? _____
3. How many bunnies? _____
4. Are there any chicks? _____

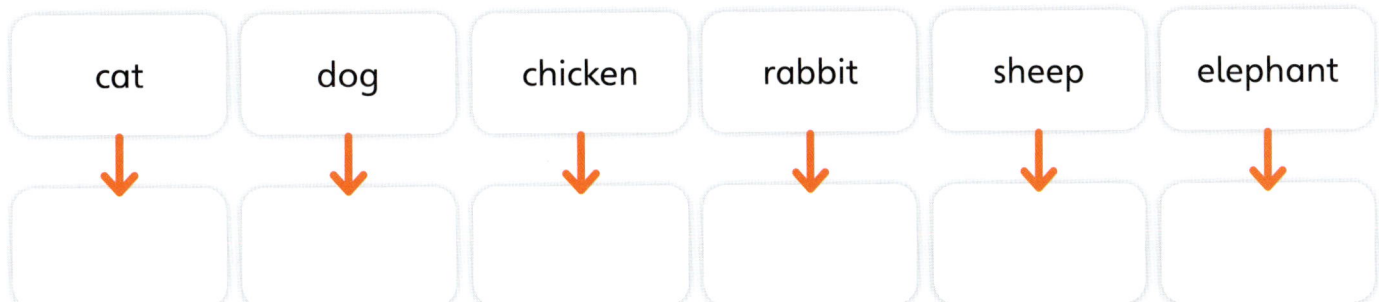

18 **Work with a partner.** Ask and answer.
What are your favorite animals? TR: B80

What are your favorite animals?

I like dogs and turtles.

My favorite animal is my cat. Her name is Missy. She is white, brown, and gray. Missy has two kittens. They are so cute! Boots is black with two white feet. Snowy is all white. I love them all.

19 **Draw and write about your favorite animal.**

My favorite animal is _____

_____

_____

20 **Work in a small group.** Talk about your picture.

NATIONAL GEOGRAPHIC

Our World

Be good to animals.

21 **Look and read.**

Give your pet food and water.

A hiker and her dog, the Himalayas

22 **Read and copy.**

I am good to animals.

23 Make a class book about animals.

Choose an animal.

Glue your picture.

Write about your animal.

Write your name.

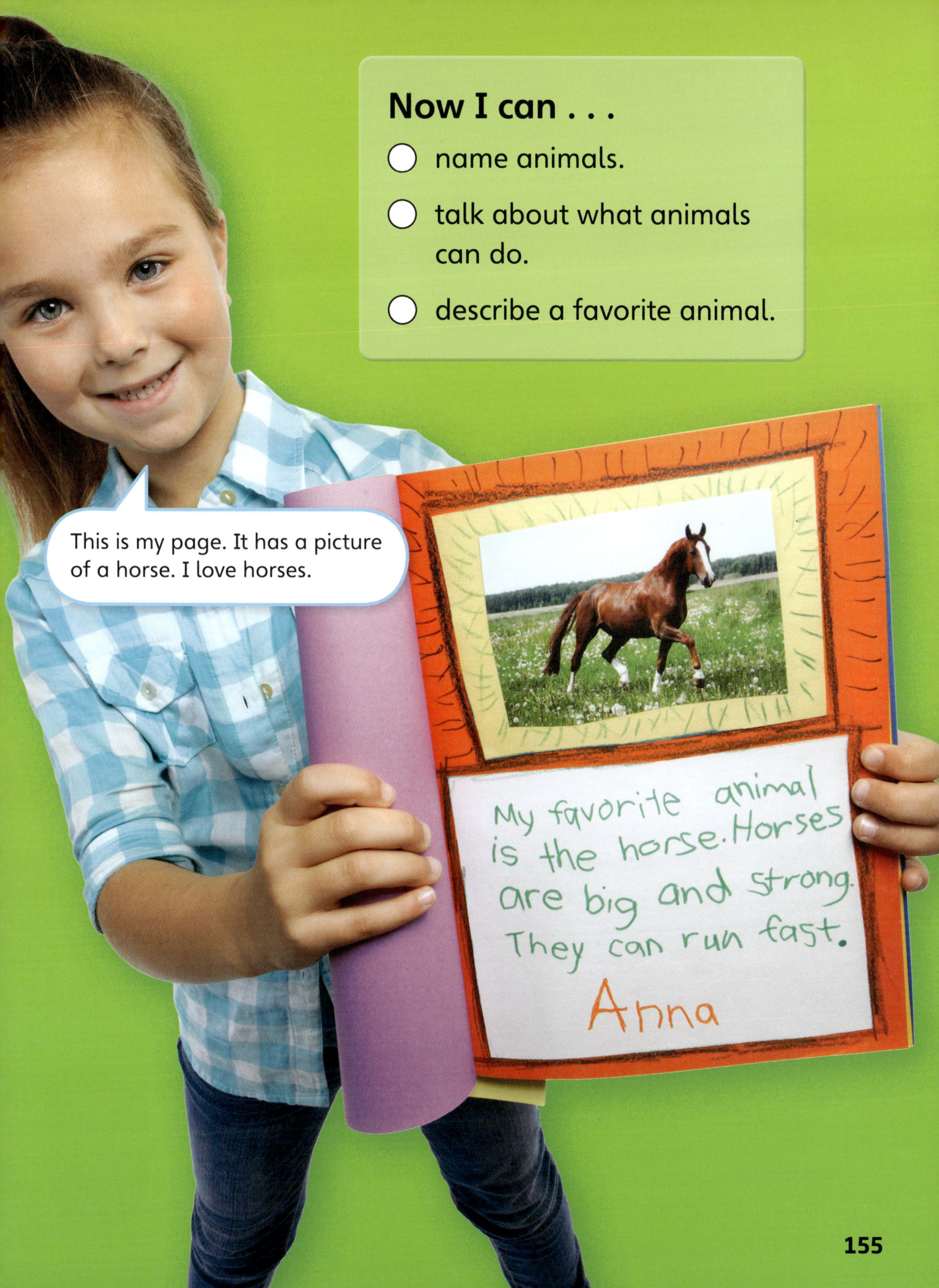

Review

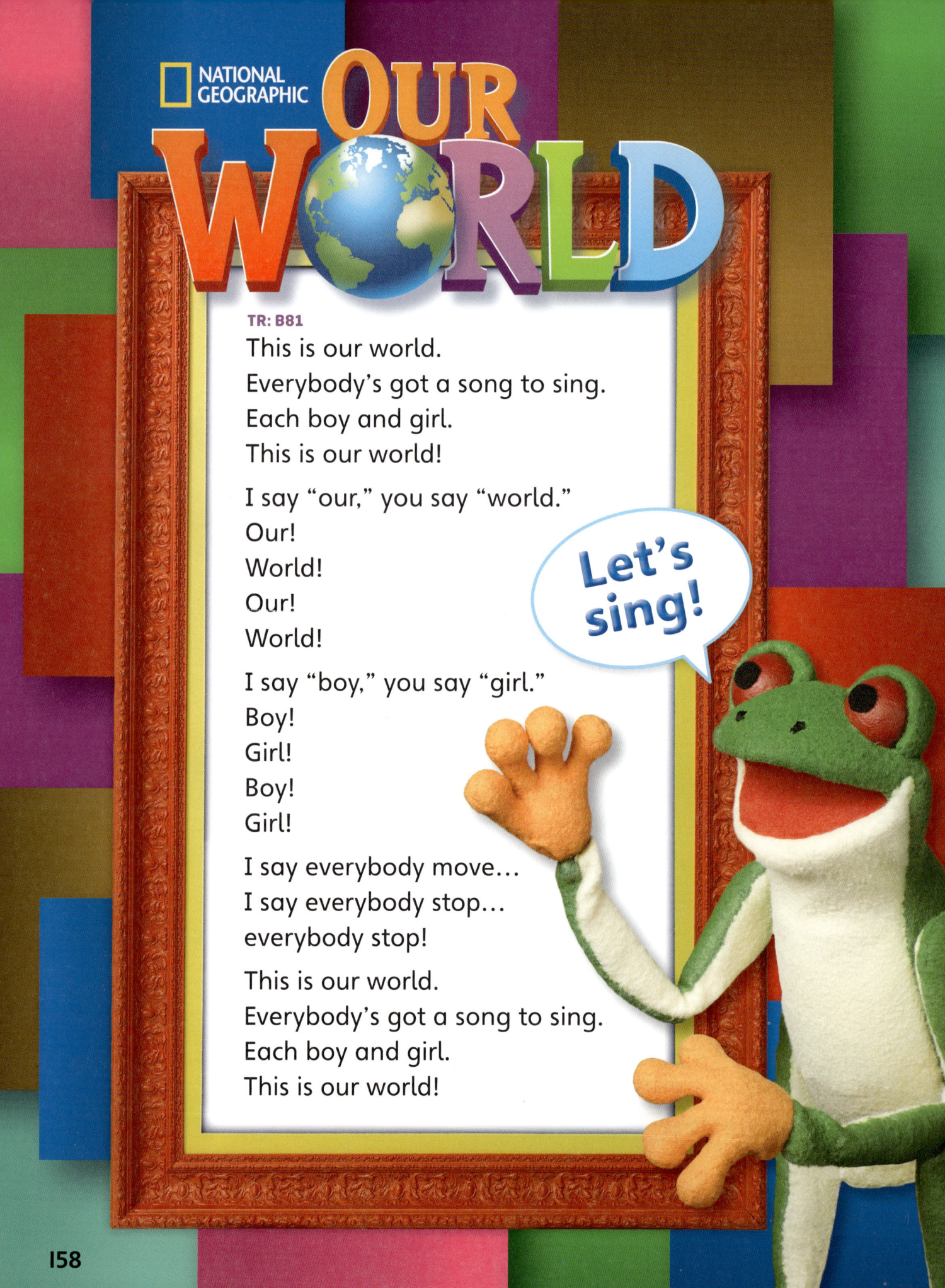

Unit I Cutouts Use with project on page 22.

Unit I Cutout Use with activity 16 on page 20.

Unit 2 Cutouts Use with project on page 38.

161

Unit 3 Cutouts Use with activity 10 on page 49.

Unit 3 Cutout Use with project on page 54.

163

Unit 4 Cutouts Use with project on page 72.

Unit 5 Cutouts Use with project on page 88.

167

Unit 6 Cutouts Use with activity 13 on page 99.

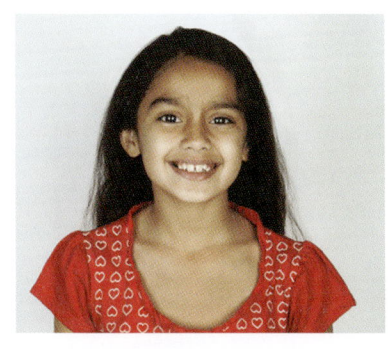
Tina

Tony

Ellen

Ben

Unit 7 Cutouts Use with activity II on page II7.

Unit 8 Cutouts Use with project on page 138.

173

Unit 9 Cutouts Use with activity 13 on page 149.

175